Animal Habitats

The Owl in the Tree

Text by Jennifer Coldrey

Photographs by
Oxford Scientific Films

Gareth Stevens Publishing
Milwaukee

Contents

Note: The use of a capital letter for an owl's name means that it is a specific *type* (or *species*) of owl (for example, Common Screech Owl). The use of a lower case, or small, letter means that it is a member of a larger *group* of owls.

A Barn Owl stands at the entrance to its nesting hole in an oak tree. Barn owls and their relatives can be recognized by their heart-shaped faces. They belong to a different family from all other owls.

In the steamy night of a South American jungle, this tropical screech owl perches, wide awake, on a branch.

A little Saw-whet Owl rests among the branches of a pine tree in a North American forest.

Tree-living owls around the world

Owls are among the most exciting and fascinating birds in the world. They are not easy to see or find because most of them are *nocturnal*. This means that they are active at night—mainly hunting for food—and spend most of the day asleep.

There are well over a hundred different *species* of owl around the world, and many make their homes in trees. Some live in deep, thick forests. Others live at the forest edge. Some make their homes among small clumps of trees in open country, and several live quite close to humans, either on farmland or among the trees of town parks and gardens.

Some owls, like the Great Gray and the Tengmalm's or Boreal Owl, live among *coniferous* trees in the forests of the cold northern parts of North America, Scandinavia, and Siberia. Those that live in milder climates, including the Tawny Owl of Europe and Asia, the North American Barred Owl, the Common Screech Owl, and the European Scops Owl, often live among broad-leaved or *deciduous* trees, or perhaps in mixed woodland. Several kinds of barn and hawk owl can be found in the wooded parts of Australia, while a variety of *tropical* owls live in the jungles of Asia, Africa, and Central and South America.

A tree offers a safe and comfortable place for an owl to hide during the day. Most owls sleep or *roost* in a tree hole or on a branch where they are well-hidden by the leaves. Their speckled coloring *camouflages* them well as they sit motionless against a background of leaves and branches. A tree also provides an owl with a good place to make a nest for laying eggs and raising its young. In addition, owls find much of their food around or under the trees, as they hunt on silent wings above the woodland floor or in the countryside close by.

The bulky rounded shape of this North American Barred Owl is typical of most types of owl.

This rare Red-chested Owlet, one of the small pygmy owls from tropical Africa, is only 6 3/4 inches (17 cm) tall.

The size and shape of owls

Some of the smallest owls are the tiny pygmy owls, found in various parts of Europe, Asia, Africa, and both North and South America. The smallest of all, the Least Pygmy Owl from South and Central America, is no bigger than a sparrow, measuring only 4 1/2 - 5 inches (12-13 cm) from beak to tail. The biggest owls are the large horned and eagle owls, which can be up to 2 1/2 ft (75 cm) tall. Between these two extremes there are many different medium-size owls.

But despite their differences in size, nearly all owls have the same basic shape and posture. They are easy to recognize because their bodies have a broad, rounded outline, and they tend to sit in a very upright position. Their large heads are joined to the body in such a way that they appear to have no neck. An owl does have a neck, of course, but it is well disguised under its thick coat of feathers. In fact, owls have such flexible necks that they can twist their heads around, almost full circle, when they want to look behind them. This looks very comical and even a little uncomfortable to us, because while their heads turn, their bodies remain perfectly still.

An owl's body is covered with a thick, warm coat of soft, velvety feathers. The outer *plumage* is usually a streaky mixture of various shades of brown and gray. The undersides of the body and wings are often paler. The short, *downy* feathers close to the body are usually pale in color, too. Some types of woodland owl, including the Tawny, the European Scops, and the North American Screech Owl, have two different "color forms"—reddish brown and gray. Gray forms are more common in northern coniferous forests, while owls of reddish-brown form live further south among deciduous trees. However, the two different forms are sometimes found together in the same *habitat*. They may even occur in the same family, just as a red-haired and a brown-haired child can be found in the same human family. There is no difference in coloring between male and female owls. Female owls, however, are usually bigger than males.

Owls have broad, rounded wings, but somewhat short, squarish tails. Their strong, stumpy legs are usually covered with feathers right down to the toes. There are four toes on each foot, and every toe ends in a sharp, curved claw. These vicious-looking *talons*, together with an owl's short, hooked beak, are signs that these birds are *predators*. They are birds of *prey,* capturing other animals such as small mammals, birds, and insects for their food.

An English Tawny Owl swivels its head to investigate a sudden noise from behind.

A close-up of the face of a Spotted Eagle Owl.

The owl's head and face

One of the most attractive features of an owl are its big round eyes, which stare out from its broad flattened face. Many owls have bright orange or yellow eyes, although some, like the Tawny Owl, have dark brown, almost black eyes. They look almost human when they blink, because they close their eyes by bringing down their upper eyelids first, as we do. This is unlike most other birds, which blink by bringing up their lower lids first. An owl's eyes are fixed in their sockets and cannot look to right or left. As we have mentioned, however, the owl manages to see around and behind itself by swiveling its head on its remarkable "elastic" neck.

At the center of the owl's "face" is a short, downcurved beak. The hooked tip is often hard to see, as it is hidden among feathers. It is an advantage for an owl's beak to be curved downward and held closely against the body, since it does not then protrude and interfere with the bird's eyesight. At the base of the bill are the nostrils, surrounded by many bristly feathers which are thought to be sensitive to the touch.

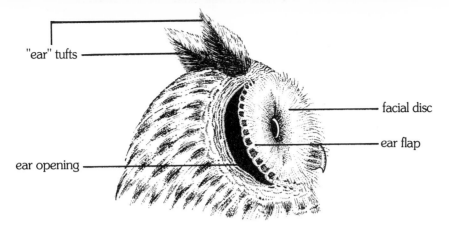

"ear" tufts

facial disc

ear flap

ear opening

The right side of a Long-eared Owl's head, showing the long crescent-shaped ear opening behind the facial disc.

Most of the feathers on an owl's face are stiff and bristly. They radiate out from the center, around the eyes, to form a kind of circular fan called the "facial disc." The ears are actually hidden behind the feathers on either side of the owl's facial disc. Owls have extremely large ears which open through long, crescent-shaped slits in the side of the head. One ear is often larger than the other and may be placed higher on the head than the opposite ear. This lopsidedness is thought to help the owl pinpoint sounds more accurately. A feathered flap of skin borders the front and back of each ear opening. An owl can open and close these flaps. In this way, it changes the size and shape of its ear openings.

Many owls, including the Great Horned Owl and the Long-eared Owl, have what look like two ears sticking out from the top of their heads. These are not ears, but simply tufts of long feathers which the owls use as signals of display. By raising or lowering their "ear" tufts, these owls can show whether they are excited, angry, or frightened.

Looking like a sleepy old man, this Long-eared Owl closes its golden eyes by bringing down its feathered upper eyelids.

7

From its perch on a tree stump, this North American Common Screech Owl turns its head sharply as it hears a sound in the darkness.

Hunters of the night

Although some owls are out and about by day, most hunt at night or at dusk and dawn, when the light is poor. Their sharp eyesight and acute sense of hearing are very important in helping them search for prey in the dark.

Owls can see remarkably well in very low light, better than other daytime birds and even slightly better than humans. The large pupils of their eyes open wide in dim light to let in as much light as possible. At the same time, the light-receiving surfaces inside their eyes are extremely sensitive to very small amounts of light. Unlike many other birds, an owl's eyes face forward and can focus together on the same object. This helps them see more clearly in semi-darkness. In order to judge the distance of nearby objects, they often bob or pivot their heads in a very amusing way.

However, even owls cannot see in total darkness. At night they rely a great deal on their sensitive hearing to help detect and catch their prey. An owl's ears are extremely good at picking up high-pitched noises, such as the squeak of a mouse or the rustling and snapping of dry leaves and twigs, as a small animal scampers across the woodland floor. The large ears are set wide apart on the skull.

This helps an owl detect more clearly from which side of its body a sound is coming. Having one ear larger, or placed higher than the other, also helps the owl hear any sound a fraction earlier on one side than on the other. This makes it easier to tell exactly where a sound is coming from. By opening and closing their ear flaps, owls can also pinpoint sounds more easily. Once an owl has picked up a noise which sounds like a tasty meal, it rotates its head until the sound is heard equally loudly in both ears. It then knows that its prey is straight ahead, right in line with the center of its face and that sharp, downcurving beak.

An owl's excellent hearing is especially useful on dark, cloudy nights, or when it is hunting among the trees in deep woodland where there is very little light. However, some scientists now doubt that woodland owls hunt at night using only their eyes and ears. They believe that the memory of its habitat is also extremely important in guiding an owl around the many twigs and branches of a pitch-dark forest. Most woodland owls hunt over the same area all their lives, so they get to know their way around, even at night. They soon learn where the best places are to hunt and find food. They also learn how to judge the distance between their favorite perches and the ground, and what obstacles to avoid when flying low through the trees in the dark.

A Little Owl flies through the night on silent wings to hunt for prey.

A North American Saw-whet Owl swoops down, with talons spread, to strike and kill a little Deer Mouse.

Catching and killing prey

As they hunt for food in the darkness, owls usually make a successful capture by using the surprise approach. Once they are within close range of their prey, they use their keen eyesight and hearing to pick up the slightest movement or sound. Then, when they have pinpointed their target, they swoop quickly and silently down to make the attack. They bring their feet forward at the last moment and strike their prey with their long, curved talons. An owl's strong legs and large clawed feet are very useful for grabbing and holding a small animal. They spread their toes wide apart, the two outer toes of each foot often held backwards to increase their grip. An owl usually kills its victim instantly by piercing it with its talons. But if this does not work, the owl will then stab its bill at the base of the skull to complete the kill. Later it may use its sharp, hooked bill to tear up the body.

The front edge of a Barn Owl's wing shows the soft, feathery fringe which helps to silence its flight.

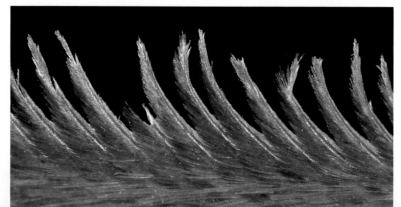

Owls catch most of their prey on the ground. Woodland owls usually sit on a low perch in a tree, waiting, watching, and listening for a tiny rustle in the undergrowth. Other owls like the Barn Owl, which hunt on more open land, fly low and scan the ground before pouncing on a victim. One or two of the smaller owls, which feed on insects or small birds, may catch these animals while on the wing.

It is almost impossible to hear an owl in flight because they fly completely silently. Their feathers have a soft, velvety surface and they are edged with a fine fringe. This helps to deaden the sound of their wings striking the air. Other animals cannot hear them coming and, because its wings make no noise, the owl itself is better able to listen for its prey as it homes in on the kill. Owls are bulky birds, but this does not mean they are clumsy in flight. They have strong, powerful wings and can fly off easily, even when carrying a struggling animal in their beaks. Woodland owls have especially short, rounded wings, which they flap slowly to help glide skillfully through the trees.

Some tree-living owls, such as the pygmy and hawk owls, hunt by day. They rely mainly on sight for capturing their prey. They are fast flyers, with longer wings and tails than nocturnal owls, and without the softened feathers to silence their flight.

Having killed its prey, this Saw-whet owl pauses for a moment before flying off with it in its beak.

A Little Owl brings home an extremely long earthworm to feed to its offspring in their tree hole nest.

Food and feeding

Owls feed on a variety of small animals, depending on where they live and what is available in the habitat at different times of year. Woodland owls, such as Tawny and Long-eared Owls, feed mainly on mice and voles. But if these are in short supply, they will eat other *mammals* such as rats, shrews, and moles. They also eat earthworms, snails, and spiders, as well as beetles and many other insects. Some owls eat small lizards, snakes, and also frogs. Even Tawny Owls have been known to catch frogs by snatching them out of shallow pools of water or, more commonly, from wet ground.

Many owls will also take small birds. Some may catch them on the wing: Others dive-bomb birds such as sparrows or starlings at their nighttime roosts, grabbing a sleeping bird as they pass. Owls that live in parks or gardens often feed on small birds, including sparrows, starlings, blackbirds, and thrushes. Sometimes the owls use their wings to beat these small birds out of the trees.

Insects are the main food of many small owls, while the large owls catch animals as big as rabbits, hares, squirrels, and chipmunks. Large owls also eat smaller owls, and they will take other birds as big as crows. There are several large day-hunting owls in Africa and Asia that specialize in catching fish. They swoop down to pluck them out of the water in their talons.

Mice and voles make a regular meal for many owls. This Tawny Owl is about to eat a Bank Vole it has just captured.

Once they have made a kill, owls usually swallow their prey head first and whole. However, they will sometimes crush the skull, or cut off the head of a larger animal, before eating it. Birds are usually eaten piece by piece, after the owl has plucked off the feathers with its beak. Once swallowed, the food is digested inside the owl's stomach. But instead of the indigestible parts passing out through the body as droppings, owls cough up, or *regurgitate*, the indigestible remains in the form of tightly packed pellets. An owl pellet usually contains bones, teeth, fur, and possibly feathers. It often contains many insect cases. Owls produce one or two pellets each day, and these are usually dropped on the ground beneath their roosting places. If an owl roosts in the same place for several days, a pile of pellets soon begins to collect. If you are lucky enough to find some owl pellets, you can discover what's inside of them by soaking them in warm water and then carefully pulling them apart. The bits of bone, fur, teeth, and other remains you find will tell you what sort of animals the owl has been eating.

You can see the bones of various small animals sticking out from these two Barn Owl pellets.

A pair of Tawny Owls roost sleepily in a hollow tree.

Courtship and mating

Outside the breeding season, male and female owls often live fairly separate lives, even though a pair may hunt over the same piece of land. As the breeding season begins, the males hoot loudly to attract a mate. The females usually reply with a different call, and a pair of owls will often sing a kind of duet together. Their different calls help male and female owls recognize each other and so come together in pairs. At first, each partner is suspicious and frightened of the other, as they are used to living on their own. A female owl may even attack a male when he first courts her, and it is only when she is sure that he is not an enemy that she will allow him to mate with her.

The courtship displays of many species of owls have never been seen. Of those that have, the male owls usually do a strange kind of dance. They often sway from side to side or bow up and down, meanwhile raising and lowering their wings or ruffling out and then sleeking down their feathers. Male Tawny Owls make grunting noises throughout and frequently snap their bills together sharply.

The female usually joins in the dance, swaying with her mate and sometimes rubbing up against him and clicking her bill with his. The male Great Horned Owl from North America has been seen to give his female a present of food—a freshly-caught rabbit—as part of his wooing.

After mating, the pair of owls stay close together, often *preening* each other's head plumage. Then they look for a place to lay their eggs. They will now roost together and display to each other frequently throughout the breeding season.

Owls do not build much of a nest, if any at all. Many tree-living owls lay their eggs in tree holes, often in the old nest of a woodpecker or squirrel. Some may even choose a nesting box put up by humans. Others, such as the Long-eared Owl and Great Horned Owl, like to nest in the open, high in the branches of a tree. They often take over an old crow's nest or the nest of a bird of prey such as a hawk or buzzard. A few owls, including the Great Gray Owl, may build a simple nest of their own, but this is nothing more than a loose platform of dry twigs. The females of one or two northern owls line their nests with some of their breast feathers, but this is not common in other species. Owls frequently pair for life, returning to the same nesting place year after year. They can begin to breed and raise a family when they are only a year old.

A pair of Great Horned Owls have laid their eggs in an open nest at the top of a tall tree in western South Dakota.

The round white eggs in this Tawny Owl's nest are safely hidden inside a tree hole.

Eggs and chicks

Owls lay white, roundish eggs. There is no need for the eggs to be speckled or well-camouflaged, because they are either hidden away in a tree hole, or safely covered by the female owl in her open nest in the tree tops. Female owls lay one egg every two days or so. Many owls lay between three and six eggs in one *clutch*. Others may produce up to 12 eggs, while many eagle owls and most tropical owls rarely lay more than one or two eggs.

The female starts to *incubate* or sit on her eggs as soon as the first is laid. This means that the chicks will hatch at different times. The last to hatch will be considerably smaller—and maybe up to two or three weeks younger—than the first and oldest chick. If the parents can supply the chicks with plenty of food, all will survive. But if food is short, only the biggest and strongest chicks will live. They will grab all the food, while the youngest will starve and may even be eaten by the rest. Although this seems cruel, it is a good way of ensuring that at least one or two youngsters will survive to carry on the next generation. When food is very scarce, owls usually lay fewer eggs, and if things do not improve, the female may abandon her young altogether because she herself is starving.

It is usually only the female that incubates the eggs. They take between three and five weeks to hatch, depending on the species of owl. The young chicks, or *owlets*, are born with their eyes closed.

This baby Tawny Owl, with its red-rimmed eyes, is only a week or two old. Its thick, fluffy down helps keep it warm.

They are covered with a thin layer of grayish-white down and are very weak and helpless. Their mother keeps them warm by *brooding* them under her body. Female owls guard their chicks fiercely and are often very aggressive at the nest. They will strike out with their talons and attack any intruder, including a human, who dares to go too near.

During incubation the female is fed by the male, who brings food back to her at the nest. He usually goes on hunting and providing food for the female and her chicks, until the young no longer need brooding. However, there are some species in which the female will also go off to hunt, once the chicks have hatched.

The female tears up the food with her bill and feeds it to the chicks. The young owlets gradually become bigger and stronger. They grow a thicker and darker coat of down. Then, later, their first true feathers start to push through. After a few weeks they are able to tear up their own food and swallow it whole.

At two weeks old, a pair of young Barred Owls huddle in a tree hollow, waiting for their parents to return with food.

17

A female North American Great Horned Owl sits close to her chicks to keep them warm in their open nest.

Growing up

By about three or four weeks old, most young owlets have developed their first real feathers. They stretch their legs and flap their tiny wings to exercise them. Soon they are ready to leave the nest. The young may climb about in the tree for a while before they venture to fly, but eventually they take the plunge and make their first flight. However, the young owlets are not yet independent and still need to be fed by their parents. They stay in the area, roosting in the trees by day and calling for food by night. Their noisy, begging calls can be heard for miles (km) around. Young owls living in open nests develop quicker and are able to fly much earlier than those in tree hole nests. Being in the open, they are more at risk from predators, so it is obviously important that they can fly and escape from danger as soon as possible.

Eventually the youngsters learn to hunt for themselves. After several months they leave their parents and move away to find their own place to live. Young owls are often reluctant to leave their home area, but the parents usually drive them away once they can fend for themselves. Some owls occasionally stay together as a family group over the winter months, but this is not very common.

Life is hard, and large numbers of young owls die in their first year. Many die of starvation because they are inexperienced hunters and cannot find enough food. Others die in the cold, while a great many are attacked and killed by predators, which include other owls. However, some do manage to survive. They are usually the ones that find a safe place to settle and make a home. Eventually they may raise a family of their own. A successful owl will usually live for about five years, but some can live much longer, up to 20 years or more.

Most owls produce only one *brood* of young a year. If there is plenty of food available, however, some may raise a second brood. Owls time their breeding so that the young hatch out when there is lots of food around. In northern countries, this will be in spring or early summer, but in the tropics, the young hatch during the rainy season when there are plenty of insects about.

The tiny wings of this Great Horned owlet are just starting to grow. You can see the remains of a dead rabbit in the nest.

Having left the nest, this young Great Horned Owl has learned to fly, but he still depends on his parents for food.

The home life of owls

Most woodland or tree-living owls stay in the same place all of their lives. Each bird sets up its own home area or *territory*—the patch of ground over which it lives and hunts. The size of the territory depends on the size of the owl and the amount of food available in its habitat. Tawny Owls have territories which can vary from about 40 to 100 acres (15 to 40 hectares). Each owl gets to know its territory well. It finds the best trees to roost and nest in, and it knows the best places to hunt for prey.

Owls guard their territories fiercely. Although a breeding pair may share the same territory, other owls are normally considered intruders and must be kept away. Owls defend their territories by calling and displaying the boundaries of their own piece of land. Each type of owl has its own particular call, ranging from hoots and screams to strange barks, whistles, snores, and coughs. Owls use their calls to express their anger, fear, or excitement. Calling is especially important at night, when owls cannot see each other, and many of their notes carry long distances through the darkness. In daylight and at close quarters, owls often communicate in other ways—by ruffling their feathers, moving their wings, or displaying their eyes or ear tufts. They presumably also recognize each other by distinctive silhouettes.

This Great Gray Owl from Canada is wonderfully camouflaged as it sits against a tree trunk in its northern home.

Long-eared Owls frequently raise their "ear" tufts to communicate with other owls.

Not all owls stick rigidly to the same home territory all their lives. Barn Owls—and others which hunt in more open country—defend a territory only in the breeding season. At other times of the year they roam more widely to hunt and look for food. Northern owls, like the Great Gray and Tengmalm's Owl, may have to travel long distances to find food when their local supplies of small *rodents* dwindle to nothing. One tree-living owl, the European Scops Owl, actually *migrates* hundreds of miles (km) south to North Africa every winter in order to find enough insects to eat.

Apart from coming together to breed, owls are mainly solitary birds. However, some are known to roost in groups during the winter. Tiny North American Saw-whet Owls often hide together in family groups in evergreen trees, while in both Europe and North America, Long-eared Owls have been found in clusters of 8 to 12, with as many as 50 counted in one small thicket. Barn Owls can be sociable too, sometimes sleeping together in large groups among a clump of trees.

A Barn Owl defends its territory by lowering its wings and thrusting its head forward, meanwhile clicking its tongue and hissing angrily.

Weasels can be enemies of owls when they climb up trees and take eggs and owlets from the nest.

Enemies of owls

Owls, although fearsome predators themselves, are not without their own enemies. Large birds of prey, including eagles and hawks, will attack and kill them, and so will other owls. Smaller owls, such as the Little Owl and pygmy owls of northern Europe and Asia, are sometimes killed by Ural or Tawny Owls, while in North America, the Great Horned Owl kills and eats a variety of smaller owls including Common Screech Owls, Barn Owls, Barred Owls, and Long-eared Owls. Large eagle owls are also dangerous killers of other owls.

The Great Horned Owl, here seen at its nest, is a frequent killer of smaller owls.

But owls do not kill each other very often. During the day they are mostly asleep and unlikely to disturb each other at their roosts. However, owls are sometimes disturbed during the day by smaller and less dangerous birds. These small birds may include chickadees, thrushes, finches, crows, jays, and magpies. If they discover a roosting owl sitting quietly in a tree, they will start to call and display in alarm. This warns other birds of the danger and more will come and join in. The small birds start to fly to and fro in front of the owl, sometimes dive-bombing it, although they never actually touch it. As they mob the owl, the birds keep up a noisy chattering and scolding, while the owl sits patiently with its eyes closed, apparently unaware of the commotion. Sometimes large crows or magpies will drive the owl away, but this is rare. The owl usually stays put and the mobbing birds eventually lose interest and go away. Although an owl is unlikely to attack them during the day, these small birds know it *can* be dangerous. By making a fuss, they warn other birds that an owl is in the area, while young birds are taught to learn and recognize the owl as an enemy.

Other animals may be enemies of owls. Stoats, weasels, and martens are a serious threat because they can climb up trees and destroy eggs and young owlets in the nest. In tropical countries, other *carnivorous* mammals, as well as snakes, may do the same.

Hunger and starvation is another cause of death in owls, especially during winter or in countries where the weather is often bitterly cold.

This Tawny Owl has died of hunger and cold during a bitter English winter.

This small gray owlet is well-camouflaged as it crouches at the entrance to its nest hole. As long as it stays still, it is unlikely to be spotted.

Escape from danger

Like other birds, owls are safe from most predators on the ground because they can fly away and seek shelter high up in the trees. Their eggs and young are also safely protected from enemies that cannot climb trees. But there is danger lurking in the trees, too, and owls are most at risk when they are roosting during the day. A roosting owl is dozy and half asleep, its senses not nearly as alert as when it is hunting at night. In order to sleep in peace, it must stay well-hidden. Some owls hide away in crevices or tree holes. Others sit on branches high in the trees, often hidden among leaves or creepers. As they sit completely still, with their eyes closed, their speckled plumage blends in well with the dappled light falling through the trees. They are especially hard to see when sitting close to a tree trunk. Here their outline seems to disappear as their coloring merges with the rough, lichen-covered bark.

A roosting Tawny Owl peers out from a tangle of ivy where it is well- hidden from enemies.

One way in which an owl may avoid being discovered is by changing its roosting place frequently. Tawny Owls do this, but many other owls return to the same place day after day. A roosting owl sits motionless and will move only if it is extremely frightened. Long-eared Owls (also some Screech Owls and other small woodland owls) stiffen their bodies into a long, thin shape when alarmed. Instead of sitting with their feathers fluffed out, they press their feathers close to the body and stretch upwards—"ear" tufts erect—until they look more like a broken piece of branch than a bird. Other owls try to disguise themselves by raising one wing in front of their body, as though hiding behind a cloak.

Sometimes owls will use their large fearsome eyes to terrify animals such as mobbing birds or squirrels. They suddenly open them wide, staring out with huge, round, black or golden-yellow orbs. This soon frightens the intruders away. Owls can be especially fierce and frightening when they are defending their nests and young from attack. They put on a dramatic display, usually lowering their bodies, raising their wings and fluffing out their feathers so that they appear twice as large as they really are. They frequently hiss, snarl, or clap their bill loudly, while those with ear tufts may raise them to try and appear more frightening. Species that nest in the open are especially savage and will strike out with their talons if an intruder comes too near. However, owls use their aggressive displays mainly to frighten and not to harm their enemies. They rarely attack other animals except when hunting for food.

This Long-eared Owl looks huge and terrifying as it puts on a threat display to frighten off intruders.

Athena, the Goddess of Wisdom, appears as an owl with arms and a spear on a small Greek pot, from the early sixth century BC.

Owls and humans

The ancient Greeks considered the owl a symbol of wisdom, and even today, people talk of owls as wise old birds. Here is an old proverb which sums up what many people once felt about owls:

A wise old owl sat in an oak.
The more he saw the less he spoke.
The less he spoke the more he heard.
Why can't we all be like that wise old bird?

But to many races of people down the ages, owls have been feared as signs of evil and the bringers of death and disaster. We can see this from the many poems and legends written about owls, describing them as messengers of doom.

Nowadays people are not quite so superstitious. Instead, many are more interested in learning about the real lives of these fascinating and beautiful birds, even though their nighttime shrieks and calls may sometimes send shivers down our spines.

A Tengmalm's or Boreal Owl has made its home in a nesting box put up on a tree in Norway.

Unfortunately, there are still some people who do not appreciate owls and who even do them harm. Gamekeepers sometimes trap and kill owls in order to protect their pheasants, grouse, and other game birds, while in many countries, hunters still enjoy shooting owls for sport. In several European countries, people use owls as lures to attract other birds so that these birds can be easily captured or shot. A large owl, such as an Eagle Owl, either stuffed or alive, is tied to a post, where it is then mobbed by smaller birds. Crows, jays, and magpies, all of which are pest birds, are caught in this way, and people also shoot and then eat the many other kinds of birds that come to attack the owl. In some countries, people cruelly use a tethered owl to bring in birds of prey, such as hawks, and falcons, so that these can be captured and used in the sport of *falconry.*

Fortunately, owls are now widely protected by law throughout Europe and in North America. Some species are not allowed to be disturbed at the nest, even by photographers—unless they have a special license! People are beginning to understand that owls really do very little harm. In fact, they can often be extremely useful, because they kill rats, mice, and numerous insect pests which cause damage to our crops.

People sometimes hurt owls without intending to. Many of the poisonous chemicals we use to spray on our crops to protect them from pests are eaten by mice and other small animals. When owls then eat these animals, the poisons build up inside their bodies. This can eventually kill them.

Even more harm is done to owls by the cutting down of trees and the destruction of their habitat. We must try to prevent further damage by protecting wild areas of woodland and by planting as many trees as possible for owls and other birds to live in. It is interesting to know that several species of owl (including Tawny Owls in Europe and Common Screech owls in North America) can live quite happily in the middle of towns and cities, providing there are plenty of trees where they can find food and shelter. It's another good reason for keeping our cities "green."

A Little Owl has a numbered metal ring put on its leg. Ringing does not hurt a bird. It is a way of marking and later recognizing an individual so that scientists can find out more about its travels and behavior.

The Tawny Frogmouth from Australia is another night hunter. Its enormously wide mouth and hooked bill help it catch insects and even seize animals as big as mice.

Friends and neighbors

Owls share their home in the trees with many other birds, including woodpeckers, jays, crows, wood pigeons, and many smaller birds. Sometimes two or more species of owl live together in the same habitat. The Great Horned Owl and the Barred Owl of North America often live close together in the same patch of woodland, but they avoid each other by keeping separate territories. Sometimes the two types of owl are of different sizes and feed on different prey, so they do not compete with each other. However, there is always the danger that the larger owls may eat the smaller ones.

A Greater Horeshoe Bat chases after a moth in the darkness.

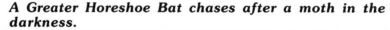

Various birds of prey, including hawks and buzzards, live and hunt in the same habitat as owls. Although they may catch and eat the same food, these birds of prey are daytime hunters and so do not interfere very much with owls' nighttime activities.

But there are other birds which come out to hunt at twilight and during the night. These are the nightjars, night hawks, or goatsuckers, nocturnal birds with large eyes and long, thin wings and tails. They fly with amazing speed and skill, catching moths and other insects in their widely gaping mouths as they dart through the air. Like bats, nightjars specialize in catching flying insects in the dark. They can live well alongside owls, since owls in general take much larger prey and catch insects mainly from the ground. Only a few of the smaller owls catch insects in flight. Australian frogmouths (related to nightjars) are more like owls because they pounce on small animals, such as millipedes and scorpions on the ground. However, they rarely take larger prey than this.

An owl's neighbors may include tree-living mammals such as bats, squirrels, dormice, galagos, or opossums, and, in the tropics, even monkeys. Some of these animals occasionally fall prey to the larger owls. Other, carnivorous animals, including weasels, stoats, martens, snakes, foxes, skunks, raccoons, and badgers, may share the same habitat as owls, as they hunt for their prey among the trees. Many of these animals hunt by night and eat the same kind of food, so they can become rivals whenever food is short.

Woodpeckers frequently share the same habitat as owls. The holes they make in the trunks of trees are often taken over later by owls.

Life among the trees

Like all other animals, owls depend on a continual supply of food for their survival. Most tree-living owls feed on a variety of small animals living within their territory. These prey animals, in their turn, feed on other small animals or plants. The diagram below shows how owls are linked with other animals and plants because of what they eat. The links are called food chains. As you will see, owls ultimately depend on plants for their survival, since the animals at the bottom of each food chain eat only plants.

Very few animals prey on owls, which means owls are usually the top predators of a food chain. Predators like owls are always present in far fewer numbers than their prey. If this were not so, they would starve to death.

Food chain

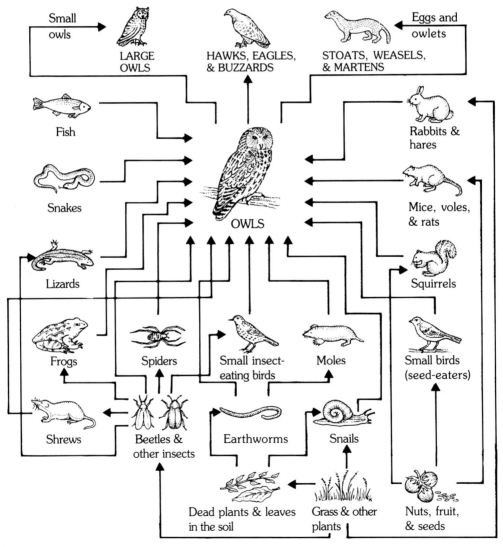

Alert and watchful in the darkness, a Tawny Owl surveys its surroundings as it perches on the broken branch of an oak tree.

Owls are well-suited to life among the trees. Even if they move into more open countryside, they return to the trees to roost and find shelter among the shady leaves and branches. Trees also offer a secluded place for owls to nest and raise their young.

Although owls are feared and avoided by many other animals living in the same habitat, a balance exists in nature so that the many different plants and animals live together and even benefit from each other. We must be careful not to upset that balance of nature so that owls and other woodland creatures will continue to survive among the trees. People have always found owls intriguing and somewhat mysterious. It is important that we do our best to protect their woodland home. Even in towns, we can encourage owls to stay by leaving old, dead trees standing, by putting up nest-boxes, and above all, by planting and not destroying trees.

Glossary and Index

These new words about owls appear in the text on the pages shown after each definition. Each new word first appears in the text in *italics*, just as it appears here.

brood............A group of young birds which have hatched from one clutch of eggs. **19**

brooding.......sitting on chicks to keep them warm. **17**

camouflage..animal disguise—the way in which the coloring or shape of an animal allows it to blend with its background so it cannot be seen. **3, 16, 20, 24**

carnivorous...meat-eating. **23, 29**

clutch...........a set of eggs in a nest. **16**

coniferous....cone-bearing (trees) with needle-like leaves, such as pine, spruce,and larch. **3, 5**

deciduous.....(of trees) shedding their leaves at certain seasons of the year, usually in autumn (except in tropics). **3, 5**

down............(downy) fluffy feathers, as on young birds. **5, 17**

falconry........the art of training and flying birds of prey, mainly hawks and falcons, to hunt game for sport. **27**

habitat.........the natural home of any group of animals and plants. **5, 9, 12, 20, 27, 28, 29, 31**

incubate.......to keep (eggs) warm so that they will hatch. **16, 17**

mammals.....animals with hair or fur which feed their young on milk. Mice,voles,and rabbits are mammals. **12**

migrate........travel to and from different areas at different seasons of the year in order to find food and survive the winter, later returning to breed. **21**

nocturnal......active at night. **3, 11,**

owlet............a young owl (also the name given to some species of pygmy owl). **16, 17, 18, 19, 22, 23, 24**

plumage.......the feathers covering a bird's body. **5, 15, 24**

predators......animals that kill and eat other animals.**5,18,19,22,24,30**

preening.......cleaning and oiling the feathers with the bill. **15**

prey..............animals that are hunted and killed by predators. **5, 8, 9, 10, 11, 13, 15, 20, 22, 27, 28, 29, 30**

regurgitate...cough up indigestible remains (or in some birds, partly digested food) from the stomach into the mouth.**13**

rodents.........a group of mammals, including rats, mice, and squirrels, with long, front gnawing teeth. **21**

roost............to sleep or rest.**3,12,13,15, 18,20,21,23,24,25,31**

species........a type of animal (or plant) which can interbreed successfully with others of its kind,but not with those of a different type. **3, 17, 25, 27, 28**

talons...........sharp, curved claws belonging to birds of prey. **5, 10, 12, 17, 25**

territory........piece of land which an animal defends against intruders. **20, 21, 28, 30**

tropical.........relating to the warm regions of the Earth lying on either side of the Equator. **3, 4, 16, 19, 23**

Reading level analysis: SPACHE 4, FRY 6, FLESCH 85 (easy), RAYGOR 7, FOG 6.5, SMOG 5.0

Library of Congress Cataloging-in-Publication Data   Coldrey, Jennifer. The owl in the tree. (Animal habitats) Includes index. Summary: Text and photographs depict owls feeding, breeding, and defending themselves in their natural habitats. 1. Owls—Juvenile literature. 2. Owls—Habitat—Juvenile literature. 3. Birds—Habitat—Juvenile literature. [1. Owls] I. Oxford Scientific Films. II. Title. III. Series.   QL696.S83C65   1988   598'.97   87-9915   ISBN 1-55532-297-2   ISBN 1-55532-272-7 (lib. bdg.) 64424

North American edition first published in 1988 by Gareth Stevens, Inc., 7317 West Green Tree Road, Milwaukee, WI 53223, USA
Text copyright © 1988 by Oxford Scientific Films.
All rights reserved. No part of this book may be reproduced in any form or by any means without permission in writing from Gareth Stevens, Inc.
Conceived, designed, and produced by Belitha Press Ltd., London. Printed in the United States of America.
Series Editor: Jennifer Coldrey. US Editor: Mark J. Sachner. Art Director: Treld Bicknell. Design: Naomi Games.
Line Drawings: Lorna Turpin. Scientific Consultants: Gwynne Vevers, Graham Martin, and David Saintsing.

The publishers wish to thank the following for permission to reproduce copyright photographs: **Oxford Scientific Films Ltd.** for front cover (Barrie E. Watts); pp. 4 left, 7, 21 below, and title page (Z. Leszczynski); pp. 10 above, 11, 17 below, 29, and back cover (Ted Levin/Animals Animals); pp. 2 and 31 (D. J. Saunders); pp. 3 left, 4 right, and 6 (M. P. L. Fogden); pp. 5, 13 above, and 20 (Joe McDonald); pp. 3 right and 20 (D. H. Thompson); p. 8 (John Gerlach); p. 10 below (G. I. Bernard); p. 23 (G. A. Maclean); p. 13 below (Tim Shepherd); pp. 15, 18, 19 left and right (Charles Palek); p. 16 (C. M. Perrins); p. 17 above (Philip Sharpe); pp. 20 above and 25 (Breck P. Kent); p. 22 above (Press-Tige Pictures); p. 22 below (Jack Wilburn); p. 24 above (Andrew Lister); p. 24 below (M. Wilding); p. 26 (Stephen Mills); p. 27 (Graham Wren); p. 28 above (J. A. L. Cooke); p. 28 below (Stephen Dalton); Bruce Coleman Ltd. for pp. 9 and 14 (Hans Reinhard); The Louvre Museum, Paris for p. 26.